A Poet's Perspective

by

Caleb Delos-Santos

Contents

No Ars Poetica?

Why can't I write about poetry?
Why is reflection an enemy?

Why do poem pros reject introspective rhymes?
Why do those gnomes punish beauty for nothing-crimes?

Who made them literary judges?
Who says noobs have to lift their luggage?

Who doesn't ponder their craft and field?
Who doesn't wonder what wonderful complexities

Or even horrible indecencies
Lead to poetry?

Well,

I don't care if those pretentious collegiate fiends hate me.
I'm going to keep writing about poetry

Because it makes me
Happy.

"Nothing" Poetry Discussing "Something."

Fiction leads to money.
Some community
snags your fantasy.
And, bam! You're wealthy.

Most literary
published "somebodies"
favor fake stories.
Fiction is easy.

Or, at least, they see
fiction like pretty
jewelry: it's pricey
but clean and mighty.

Meanwhile, poetry
is weak and dirty.
It's poor and lonely.
But, it mirrors me.

It's loose and puny
but bleeds honesty
and vivacity.
It's reality.

It might be
worth nothing.
But, at least,
poetry is me.

A Whistle in the Wind.

My rhymes are fast snaps in a timeless breeze,
a flimsy note in shelves of melody.
My tiny cough can't take on the long wheeze
and sneeze literary history.

Somehow, great saint-like writers snore from graves,
outshouting me and promising young peers.
Even the deaf can feel those famous waves,
but our refrains can't flick the clearest ears.

Sure, some new pros might solo in textbooks
but only those whose puny half-beats seek
white men, mothers, and *TikTok*ers, the crooks
who never let the best fresh poets speak.

Aeolian Harps still rhapsodize today,
but storms make sure the world can't hear them play.

Comparing Poetry.

Most people treat poetry like toilet paper.
They adamantly unravel its mysteries
and desperately reach for its bottom-releasing
properties. They crave the thick yet soothingly slick

paper that smoothly saves bums from disgusting states.
But when those junkies finally clench bowel-quenching cloth,
they thoughtlessly shove it up their ass, snatching its
Mastery so they can mindlessly recite it

to other dumb assholes, and then instantly flush
its existence into society's sewage tubes.

To be fair, some poems deserve this since they're
basically an apple with shimmering crimson
skin and moistly nutritious flesh fashioned from fair
and mighty trees with English degrees. Such poems

blow most away with scrumptious one-liners. But once,
customers chomp away the fabulous fat, they
unveil the false fruit's empty core and deadly seeds.
But, true poetry deceives like a tootsie pop.

Its shell is hardly sweet and incomplete. Yet, its core
is a needed treat and something others must adore.

Sunsets+Green.

Sunsets.
When people get
lively and belt songs for
those righteous rays, they praise the Core
Colors. Orange, Yellow, Red, and sometimes
Light Purple hear delightful cheers. But, no one chimes
for Green. It's rare and hard to spot. Yet, it
flares fearless, flawless, and free, spits
at eyes, and glows just right.
Green is just like
Poetry.

A Poet at Work During Church.

Church is a great place for poetry.
Even though church-goers stare "kindly,"

They don't notice anything. They peak
At my scribbly notebook and think,

"He must be writing down the preacher's wise thoughts."
Those drones see a committed Christian robot,

Not an Agnostic rebel poet,
Critiquing white men on "bright" pulpits.

They throw me a *Harry Potter* cloak,
And I use it to silently poke

Their "welcoming" cult with biting poetry.
And, no matter how hard my strikes are,

They'll never notice me.

But,

Do you think
That's a good thing?

Years Ago.

Years ago,
Instead of worshipping,
I wrote poetry.

Years ago,
As peers mumbled melody,
I rhymed poorly.

Years ago,
Once churchlings raced to note-taking,
I riffed pitifully.

Years ago,
While a preacher screamed eternally,
I refrained plainly.

Years ago,
Instead of rising for final praisings,
I sat to complete my crappy infant poetry.

Then,
When their singing and my writing finally ended,
I stood and left.

Yet,

Years ago,
Despite my non-participating,
I admired every gathering

Since
Every time I exited the building,
Something holy left my body.

Even now,
After every Sunday morning,
That transcendent energy,
Whatever it might be,
Leaves me longing.

Maybe,
Despite what too many religious critics think,
Divinity can reach anyone doing anything,

Including
A crazy
Anti-worshipping
Baby

Writing poetry.

A Sociable Poet.

They don't speak to me
about poetry.
Most say
they "praise" words in key.
Some even "love" free
verse. They
all gleam and "agree."
But, I never see
them stay.

Artist vs. Artist.

Some artists try
to amplify
life's speckled sky.
They magnify
their eyes and fly.
Some artists tie
them down and dry
each dreaming eye.

Thoughts From an Unwanted Location.

I don't want to be here. I wish I could
Escape this Hellish room. Although, it would
Be Hell to sit in any other place.
It doesn't matter where I am. Each space
Palms my head and then suffocates my mind.
These populated areas design
A calculated torment for my thoughts.
I stutter, shift, and shake. To help, I jot
Down pointless words with my pen. They serve as
My air. They're the last life-reserve I have,
But my love for creative writing is
Dying. And, life flattens without its fizz.
My writings will leave soon, and when I do
Run out of air, will I die in this room?

On the Loved.

I don't know who that Shakespeare fellow was.
I won't go round and say I ever will.
Though, "they" say loving him is all the buzz.
So, pray today "they" swallow my fat pill.
Look, we get it. The man was quite the God.
Books see to it that all still worship him,
But does anyone think such love is flawed?
Just 'cause I ask does not mean he's dim
In my mind, but love for his work should not
Then coincide with loving one whom those
Alive did not see with their eyes. We got
No prize like that, just his good rhymes and prose.
I'm done, but I'll claim, just before I go,
I don't love any person I don't know.

Hello, Reader.

Is this poem good?
No? Tell me. How would
You know? You only see
nature poetry,

ancient rhymes, and lines
about protest signs.
You pompous hacks chew clichés
like a bag of *Lay's*,

claiming their crummy
airy bits have beauty
and prove exquisite mastery.
Then, you peek at me

and dare say I stink?
My poetry reeks
with bite-heavy creativity
even when I lean

into your preferences.
And yet, you hate me.

You don't know poetry.
If you did, you would search

for truly new poets
and not copiers of those before

or toads who hardly know
what the term "prose" means…

Please,

at least,
look at me
and see
that I
am trying.

Strained Sunday Scratching.

My sweaty Sunday wrist looks worn out. It
can hardly crinkle and shift is grey paint
brush from left to right. This husked hand will faint
if it proceeds past one piece. A health kit
of water, lotion, or cloth could equip
it with some of its boundless but quite quaint
skill. Yet, this lonely palm doesn't know one saint
containing limb care. It should probably quit.

Yet, despite its dying state, this wrist works on
since it lacks the wit to do anything
else. All it can do is scratch paper songs
of graphite chalk. The world might never sing
them. Yet, these tired touch-tips still spend long
nights striving to create one great writing.

This Year.

The man just runs. No fuss. One plan. Yet, can
He still find the will to go on the long
And sickening trip that rips wickedly
The souls of most? Will he soon host his goal?

He feels the wind spin and peel 'round his chest.
His prep for the race gives his best steps grace.
His body's always ready for the run.
What's not is his mind's lot of rotting thoughts.

Will he stand tall and win or fall to sin?
The sin, which sits within him lit like a
type of bright light, just burns and turns all life
To death, all breath to wind, all cheers to tears.

He knows sin's strength, its ever growing length.
Though, that's not the rot he now fears… Each year
He tries this trip. Each year he dies to "It."
Not sin but "It," whose skill and wit kills him.

The "It" does live within him too, it's true,
But while sin just destroys, "It" will employ
Lies and tricks, which stick to the Man's fine mind
And make him wonder why he even tries.

To win or sin takes will, which "It" breaks and kills.
"It's" here… He feels "It" stealing his quick pace.
His heart wades. His soul's passion fades. He's done.
"Next year, I'll win," He states. Till then, "It" waits.

Non-Growing Poetry.

Tell me.
Does Poetry
do anything? The Sea
breeds kelp. Could Poetry bury
one tree?

No Poem Today.

I have nothing to say today,
No witty hot takes to display.

I have no form for these stanzas,
No meter extravaganzas.

I have no rap-happy rhymes here,
No snide lines that strike like a spear.

I have no mastery to reflect,
No brilliance for you to inspect.

I have no emotion to show,
No empathy for you to stow.

If this is for no one, nothing,
Then why am I even writing?

Betty White Died.

Betty White died. She did not reach
one hundred. Two weeks more, she would have breached
that age-wall only few healthy lucky lads breathe passed. Some
famous friends sneaked
over that steep timely wall, but none earned the climb more than
Betty.

Betty White died. She did not see
passed the 2021st Earth-seam.
She did not view the end of an awkward year where people
scaled for a dream
too high. They begged the world to respawn from sickness and
quarantine.

Betty White died. She did not get
another chance to save the world and set
future standards for youngins so they might one day pass all
walls without a fret.
Like tons, she did not vault New Year's Eve and likely died with
regret.

A Dormant Poet.

I won't lie.

My flow might
die, choked, like
tight clothes. I
fight. Though, time
might grow my
plight. So, I
cry most nights.
I know why.

I don't write.

Define Artists.

Artists are a paper clip
on the floor. Some try to dip
and pick them up. Most slide by
saying, "why risk a bad trip?"

Artists are an exit sign.
No one needs them. Yet, they shine
and scream like Jesus, thinking
songs and blinking are divine.

Artists are a bumblebee.
They sting everything yet flee
fast, fearing smashed wings and God.
They fly flawed, unawed, but free.

How to Write a Sublime Sonnet.

Begin with bold but broad "strong thoughts." Then, rhyme
your lines' ends every other time. Although,
Iambic Pentameter sucks, each time
you break it, Shakespeare fearers' hate-tears grow.

Conclude each stanza with four lines. This is
what poem-douchebags call a Quatrain. By
the seventh line, describe activity. "Chris
awoke and skipped." Give verbs like that a try.

Make sure to add some classy pretty tricks,
like assonance, alliteration, odd
improper nouns, like "stakes" instead of "sticks."
When lost, try sideways thoughts on Mom or God.

Then, end your work with an insightful line,
and recognize your sonnet's fine design.

An Apology for Apathy.

I am not sorry for my apathy.
I see why we cling to caring. But please,
Fleshy things do not matter much to me.
Some souls here and there I dare call buddy.

But, not too many. Enemies are fun.
Yet, tons are dumb, dull, and full of one
Thought. Animals can manage more funds
For clever thinking, meaning humans suck.

It's funny. I am an apathetic
Asshole. And yet, who could bet one set flick
Of caring would snap my heart, like a stick?
What damned devastation deadened this prick?

Who the hell came and made this hate-heart swirl
With empathetic care? It was a girl.

On Art.

They were right, those Romantics. Mountains are
Beautiful. Their toned greens and rough molds
Are quite the sight. It's good art, but it's far
From God's best work. That title's now been sold.

My love beats all God's creatures, plants, and hills.
She's glorious with her toned olive skin.
Just one look at her hazel-touched eyes fills
Me with a peace and joy that makes me grin.

And, she's more than quite the sight. Her insane
Brain and soul are full of fun thoughts and laughs.
Though it's true, she's a rough mold, all the pain
She starts, she ends. That proves to me we'll last.

You were right, Romantics. God's art is blessed,
But the art I, alone, call mine is best.

Raw Thoughts as She Draws.

I wish I could craft the creations I see
her wink to life with ease. I'm speechless when she
builds breathtaking art pieces for fun. Her free
beauties astound me.

How does she do it? Her eyes spot such lovely
sparkles in her mind. Then, she tinkers on these
papers until all hearts leap. One glance gives glee
and hope to any.

I once feared I'd have to drop art and all things
for a simple, boring life. She proves to reach
for fair wealth and settled health sucks. Instead, we
should create our dreams.

A Black and White Dark to Light Writing.

As I try to write mighty thoughts on dark
depressing evil feelings, a bright spark
fights starkly against intense offenses
to my once cold soul. This untamed fire fenced

My freezing fiending mind. And now, my head
Swarms with warm thoughts that thaw my heart. Instead
of iced pain, nice flames flare my fleeting days.
She is to blame, that mighty bright light that paves

The way for fun sunny love for ages.
She has shaped and changed my lifelong wages.
Since she made my small, sick, and stilled soul stir,
All my poetic pieces point to her.

Replying to My Love.

Last night, while sighting moonbeams, you sighed,
Love.
You hunted my exhausted eyes and cried,
Love.

While shedding, you pressed, "why do you want my
Love?"
Then, blankets ate you. I could not reply,
Love.

But now, tonight, my rhymes will tell you why,
Love.
Your feral feasting Love chomps my insides,
Love.

It daily stalks my heart and splits it wide,
Love.
But, thanks to such Love, I am still alive,
Love.

Because you monstrously brought me to life,
Love,
Your Love is something I will not defy,
Love.

Code 53X.

I've never written a poem on sex
Since dwelling on it scares me. But, to form
Opinions, I write. So, here goes, I guess.
Sex is a need. That's why people use porn.
But, what is this need? What makes sex the best?
When "satisfied," why do we still need more?

Sex is a bond connecting life and death.
When making love, we are our most alive,
And we can, in turn, make life in this fest.
Empowerment, community. We strive
For these in life and find them during sex.
Yet, when we're "done," we're not the same, we die.

Sex is a lesson no one can resist
That teaches us how it feels to exist.

I Am a Blue Stage Light.

Though
I float
fairly low,
no
one knows
I glow
here. I am toed
to a barely sowed
cord on a stage this COVID-slowed
school can hardly afford. No
snow
shows
up here.

But, rain does come through the tears
of weird
talented yet talon peddling peers,
who steer
productions for silent cheers.
These fiends only appear
because I provide them light.

My
bright
blue hue might
not mic
mini-mouths or fight
make-up flaws. And yes, those uptight
trite

white
spotlights
might matter more than me. But each day, I
will still shine
on.

Not
long
from now, songs
will cease to reach my long
gone
and popped
bulbs. Someday, simulated dawns
and set-made lawns
will stop
inflating my over-drawn
view.

Too
few
stage lights chew
away their awaited fate in the trash hew.
But, before tomorrow's tech crews
cue
for my God-construed
end to ensue,
I will hang true
and blue.

Hangy.

What makes personality?
I named a hanger "Hangy"
once. My fading grey Sharpie
labeled his vivacity.

What makes personality?
After I named him, Hangy
dangled "rebelliously"
in reverse and swerved lightly.

What makes personality?
One day, Hangy seemingly
tackled my side. Soon, "silly"
pranks like that happened daily.

What makes personality?
As I escaped Home to see
if films were my destiny,
Hangy waved, "don't forget me."

"What makes personality?"
I don't know. Go ask Hangy.

A Left Lying Gwawdodyn.

I write positively on the Left.
I don't totally know why. I guess
I don't tend to lie about Life when Right,
and Death torments me less when I'm West.

While I'm here, Time's jests are hardly pests.
And, the Left lacks the Lord's messy tests.
Joy's coy creeds don't bleed bereaving nuke-weeds.
On the Left, I don't hold Life's cold crest.

The Left thinks I'm a dainty saint blessed
by God, a holy wholesome bright guest.
The Right thinks I'm white haughty rotting blight
from man's rancid infective conquest.

I wish the Left's nest always impressed
my depressed writing-eggs. Yet, the best
it can do is weekly for now at least.
But one day, I'll stay here on the Left.

Poetry in Response to Bigotry.

I'm not gay,
but I must say
it's strange
that they
claim
I must state
or somewhat feign
that I'm straight.

I'm not bi,
but I
don't like
the hate-loving line
they've tried
to hide
with "kind"
lips and lies.

I'm not queer,
but I fear
that their Jesus-geared
grace-spears
have pierced
my fierce
yet fragile peers,
condemning them to tears.

I'm not gay,
bi, queer, trans, ace,

or non-binary. But, those great
parties have made
their way
to this *Coke*-soaked poem page,
and they
can stay.

My Stand Against the Ants.

When an
evil band
of vamping
day-three sieging ants
rammed
my silver soda can
and
swamped the one clean serene tan
desk I had in my cluttered crammed
apartment, I ceased my trance.

I realized Stan,
the university's Batman
of ant
assassination, would not reply to my spammed
battle cry since he was a fan
of the Maintenance Branch
House-call Ban.
Knowing I was alone, I enacted my last-chance
plan…

I jammed
to my tiny kitchen, glanced
at and
fastly snatched the off-brand
paper towels and dish soap, and
pranced
to the war zone to take my final stand.

I manned
the bubbly bombs and rained a strand
of acidic disinfectant airstrikes. The ants
scrammed.

Before my insect enemies could land
a counterattack, I stamped
a paper towel atop their phalanx. Wham!
Despite their mighty grand
high-numbered clan,
the ants
did not stand
a chance.

I damned
Most of them. And,
those unwarrior-like AWOLers who ran
in retreat, probably flew further than
France
and
hid in holes punier than pieces of sand.

With my masterful hands,
I slammed
those scarlet foes better than
I slap ham
on my discount pan.
And,
best of all, not one ant
danced
in my pants.

Thanking a Flea.

Come here, little flea.
No. I'm not angry
but the contrary.

Thanks for being here
and making it clear
clean sheets aren't near.

You, my dirty lord,
blotched the "polished" floor
my "pure" roommates bore.

They seek luxury.
You bleed honesty
and trashy beauty.

Also, sweet "pest," you
prove Life can thrive through
kept or unswept rooms.

Living can be fair
with stained homes, clothes, hair.
So, why should we care?

I Hate the Rimas Dissolutas.

I struggle with this poem form.
The Rimas Dissolutas kicked
my ass last night. It took me way
too long to find each stanza's rhymes
and add non-spastic letter pairs.

Before, I forged works like a worm.
I slithered through verse-shit and picked
exquisite fruit. I frayed lame clay
and made amazing written chimes.
But now, I've floundered down the stairs.

This Rimas Dissolutas-germ
has punched my pancreas and flicked
away my gifts and training. Pray
you never try this from. Some grimes
can only hide disguised dried pears.

The Rehearsal Rain Parade.

Cloudy hues intrude
a dance interlude.
Droplets form. Pretty
players dodge drippy

beams and humming trees.
They try harmonies
under shelter, but
their vocals can't cut

through the rain's metal
screams. "It won't settle,"
a director cries
as rehearsal dies.

An Outsider at an Acting School.

I'm stifled to see
so many
Dreamers
dance for life on a frightening stage
as they pray
for Destiny to please pick them as their
Life-time partner.
They want parts, praise, picture shows,
Power.

I recline in my assigned
rehearsal seat, staring at
beautifully built figures, picture-perfect performers
with Western-winning complexions,
comparing my scrawny, sunken, stupid body,
and I feel
Envy.

Questions From a Body Weight Induced Panic Attack.

Why am I pacing?
How do I keep spacing?
What shape am I chasing?
Which slabs am I macing?

Why am I shaking?
How is my weight aching?
What gnome am I breaking?
Which myths am I waking?

Why am I hating?
How can I stop rating?
What love am I grating?
Which try am I dating?

Thoughts on Opening Night.

Theatre slaughters priests.
Theatre swallows dreamy feasts.
Theatre swaddles Beasts.

These Days Are Difficult.

These days are difficult.
A hundred soda cans.
Incinerated pans.
A kid-disguised adult.
These days are difficult.

Shift-melted fast-food hands.
Cracked roofs and broken fans.
A lock without a bolt.
These days are difficult.

Abandoned dreams and plans.
Cheap shrinks on preacher stands.
A life without revolt.
These days are difficult.

A Cursing Curtal Sonnet.

Why can't I cuss in poetry? Why do
dicks bastardize supposed "shitty" words,
deporting them to Satan's sexy list?
Why do entitled "classy" assholes glue
obnoxiously "sublime" shithead word-turds
to papers, laptops, schools, and kids? I'm pissed
that pure-bread poet bitches stitch the "mutt"
tag to my works and flee, like bloody birds.
If those damned fowls stayed, they'd see Jesus-kissed
sterility in these cocked- You know what?
Fuck this…

What You Need for Fame.

You don't need knowledge.
You don't need smarts.
You don't need college.
You just need to look the part.

This.

This loneliness is creeping into my
Heart. Even though my mind will kill its lies,
My fragile heart won't overcome the pain
That comes with thinking no one loves you. Shame
Will petrify my hands. They will not reach
For others' help. To live, my eyes will leach
Onto distractions. Entertainment will
Invade my sight, but games and shows won't fill
The bullet wounds in my chest that self-doubt
Will fire. My chest and stomach will shout out,
"You're too fat. That's why no one loves you. Starve
Yourself to end this loneliness or… Carve
Your wrists with a knife." Then, my wrists will crave
A deadly pain. My legs will try to save
Me from the cuts, but they won't run fast enough.
This loneliness will damn me to the dust.

Old Reacher.

I need to reach more
dreams before my floor
pins me
for each limb I tore
while tiny, before
a tree,
leaf, or grocery store
moves and reaches more
than me.

On *Stranger Things.*

Stranger Things is fun,
but I despise one
part: those actors
are too young. Factors

spawned by God have shot
them to fame. I thought
I would reach that mark
by now. Did my "spark"

sink? Was it unfit?
They said it would split
this land like magma
and pop like plasma.

Instead, "Eleven"
flares millions again,
while I drown and try
to rectify my

Snuffed
Life.

An Ice Cream Spoon's Lament.

I used to scoop for
gooey gold to pour
into a craved face.
Now, I'm on the floor,

a room cleaning chore.
I was a sweet spore
for peace, joy, and grace
but not anymore.

The Shattering of a Spoon.

Once, I wrote a poem about a pink ice cream spoon.
I personified the tiny guy, and he lamented his spent existence.
Another time, I mixed those slick rhymes with a lo-fi tune,
Hoping *TikTok*-poems would bring me publicity through relatability or
even resistance.

Yesterday, I spotted another puny spoon on the smudgy Huntington
pier.
However, unlike the first pink scooper, some Hi-Top stomped this
circle-knife.
My West-Coaster-mind overlooks trash. So, I abandoned the
smashed plastic spear.

But today,
As I reflect in rhyme,
I wonder…

What does that pink spoon's splattering mean for my poetic life?
Should I expect my career to end soon?

Prophecies mostly reveal future boons
But can bring unappealing dooms too.
What kind of prophecy have I received?

Why do you laugh?
Do you think I'm crazy?
Go ahead. Call me a loon.

But first, tell me.
If people see poetry
In the electrical splitting of a tree,

Why can't I see prophecy
In the shattering of a spoon?

Suicide Looks So Lovely in Cursive.

"Suicide looks so lovely in cursive."
"Um, what?" Eugene caressed her chilly cheek.
"Well, it makes it look peaceful or passive."
"Oh, I'm not worried. I just think it's bleak."

"Why do you think it's bleak? You know it's been-"
"I know." His hand transitioned to her wrist.
"I was anxious last week, okay? You win."
"Should I be worried?" He beheld her cyst.

"I'm not worried. I promise it was just-"
"Don't worry. Just keep writing. I'm not mad."
"I swear, it'll be history soon. Once-"
"I know." He kissed her head. "I'm not your dad…"

"Thank you… You know, I like your name in cursive too."
"I'd hope so." He embraced her. "I love you."

A Poem Past My Prime.

I hate this poem since it makes no sense.
First, I talk of young wintry days gone by,
where the sun shined over my summer pool.
Then, I try my best in-text rhymes each line. next, I

soar straight through structured stanzas and go back
to the good old days. I miss my first poem
notebook. I tested true treats in that black
leather piece. Wait, white? Were there two? I flow them
together in my mind. I hate
this mess.
God once blessed me with timed rhymes and lines for…

All. Oh, God. I Can't Recall.

Why CaN't I Find My W0rds?

When was I Young?
When was my Prime???

Goodbye…

Goodbye.

A chill fills the still gloomy room. A boy
Died. He now lies inside a dead-tree box
Displayed for jaded family, friends, and foes.
Their woes transform the stone church into sand.

But, why do they mourn? How did he die? It
Was suicide, a razor to his wrist.
His poor fist listened to his mind and signed
His arm. In turn, his act caged his young age.

Such deals appeal to some: becoming one
Forever young. Yet, that's not why he died.
Life's hardships stifled his dreams. They seemed so
Real. He thought they'd unfurl in this cruel world.

But soon, his age betrayed him and made him
See the cheap fleetingness of living in
This worthless earth. Not one has purpose here.
He feared death. Yet, the best of earth is worse.

He used to dream of spotlights beaming bright
On his face as he raced across a stage
In song and dance for long committed fans.
He wanted to chase that goal, despite the toll.

But, days on stage soon emptied him as well.
Hell didn't come close to the pain and stress
That theatre put on his chest. Even rest
Would fail to calm him. Nothing stopped his qualms.

Too often, each day would fill him with dread.
He melted to the pelting stress that came
With life, school, work, friends, lovers, family too.
They all fell to his blind and anxious mind.

But, what set off his awful act? He lost
That perfect girl who once gave his mind wings.
Too bad his brashness cost him her. He fell
Again and died this time since he lost her.

The service ends. None want to spend their day
Just praying in a grey room. They rush him
To his tomb. Now, the dirt will hush and doom
His thoughts. They'll be forgotten, left to rot.

When I Stop.

When I stop racing,
I taint my "steady"
routine
but treat anxiety.

When I stop chasing,
I forfeit money
and "esteem"
but buy serenity.

When I stop,
"everything"
freezes
besides
relief.

But,

does stopping
make me
happy?

Goodbye, Reader.

Decide. Does this satisfy
you? I stalk the thoughts beside
your thumbs. What you ratify
I suckle and pump. Decide.

Please…